DOWNLOAD THE AUDIOBOOK

Don't just read it, put it into action! Just to say thanks for purchasing my book, I would like to give you the audiobook and a digital copy of the Action Plan, 100% FREE! Simply Visit:

www.benweaver.org/relationshipbonus

PRAISE FOR RELATIONSHIPS ARE EVERYTHING

"I wish I would have had this book 12 years ago before I got married, before I became a dad, before I grew up. It would have changed everything."
— Jeff Goins, best-selling author of *The Art of Work*

"A transformational life crisis struck for me in 2001. Realizing at this point purpose and meaning are the central ingredients for a quality life, however, without amazing relationships this goal is elusive. Ben shares core principles here in his latest book, *Relationships Are Everything*, that prepares you to flourish in all of your relationships."
— Aaron Walker, Coach/Author/Speaker *View From The Top*

"In *Relationships Are Everything* Ben intertwines personal experience, humor, gut checks, and his passion for developing Godly men to shed light on areas we guys often intentionally overlook … This book gives practical, tangible methods that guys can employ to deepen their relationships, adding meaning and purpose to their lives, helping them become the men they want, need, and are called to be. Take his advice- DON'T. SUCK.'
— Nick Tilley, Adventure Guru, Founder of BackPackU

"As a guy, we can get so focused on getting our stuff done that we forget about relationships and how important they are in our lives. Ben reminds of just that, but will also will teach you how to thrive in them. Guys, we desperately need this help. *Relationships Are Everything* is a game changer in helping you to build strong relationships. Read it. Digest it. Put it into action."

— Chad Jeffers, Author and Creative Coach, 25notes.com

"We all know we need help at relationship-ing. But few dare to share such rich wisdom and honest stories of failure and success. Thank you, Ben for creating such a fresh, helpful book."

— Mike Loomis, Entrepreneur & Author Coach, mikeloomis.co

RELATION-SHIPS ARE EVERYTHING

How To Not Suck at Relationships
& Make a Dent in This World

BEN WEAVER

Relationships Are Everything: How to Not Suck at Relationships & Make A Dent in This World

Copyright © 2018 by Ben Weaver, benweaver.org

All rights reserved. No part of this book may be reproduced or utilized in any form or by any means, electronic or mechanical, or by any information storage and retrieval system-except for brief quotations for the purpose of review, without written permission from the author.

Cover Design: Morgan Mechelke
Interior Design: Pamela Hodges
Content Editing: Christy Pitney

You are welcome to use a short excerpt of this book for review purposes.
For other queries, contact info@benweaver.org

This is for the Monday Night Crew
– Jonathan, Nick, Todd, Corey & Shane.
You are greater than friends.
You are my brothers.
May we spend the rest of our lives celebrating wins
and not sucking at relationships.

TABLE OF CONTENTS

Foreword 11
by Kenny DeShields

Notes about the Printed Edition

Introduction. 15

Chapter 1 21
Begin Living as if Relationships Are Everything

Chapter 2 35
Embrace Pain as Part of the Process

Half Time. 49

Chapter 3 53
Stop Consuming People. Start Investing in Them.

Chapter 4 67
Vulnerability Is Your Mojo

Conclusion 83

About the Author 87

14- Day Action Plan 97

FOREWORD

I used to ask myself "Why do I care so much?" I thought I was "weird" for being a guy who often wondered how my friends were doing throughout the day. Do other people think like this? Why was I the one doing most of the texting, calling, making plans to hang out? It was exhausting and disappointing, to say the least. So, I stopped…or at least I tried to.

Through countless conversations with God and trusted friends, I broke ties with the lie that I was a weirdo but a passionate man who longed for an authentic connection with others. That's not a feminine quality but a key component of who we, as human beings, are at the core, and it's something I should embrace.

Fast forward to my family's transition to The Crossing in Chesterfield, MO where I accepted a full-time job to become an Artist-in-Residence. My musical dreams were coming true, but now it was time to make new friends in a very different culture from what I was used to. Insert Ben Weaver.

I was a "Ben fan" before I really knew him. I saw that he was a guy blogger who had these amazing adventures, took exercise seriously and was just a cool guy. I wanted to be his friend! LOL.

Ben and I would meet weekly to process how work was going, pray for one another, and share dreams and aspirations. It was cool and refreshing to have someone else in my "new world" pour back into me and allow me to pour into him.

When Ben presented the idea for this book, I was in from the title. My marketing mind said, "There's something to this." As he continued to explain how this book would help single guys, in particular, not suck at relationships, my heart swelled. How I wished someone would've written this when I was single. But what's even more amazing is that this book is for all men…. period. We need this.

We need other men to help us be our authentic selves. As you comb through the pages of this book, take time to reflect not only on the words but the heart behind them. Let them seep deeply into the pores of your soul and allow it to change how you think, feel and act from the inside out.

Kenny DeShields, Singer/Songwriter

A NOTE ABOUT THE PRINTED EDITION

When I first released *Relationships Are Everything* I never anticipated bringing it to print. My goal from the beginning was to get it into the digital hands of guys all over the world. I never once thought it would come to life on real paper.

One of the benefits of having a digital book is you get to be extra creative with how you deliver it. For me, this was inserting small videos throughout the book that you could click on and watch to hear more of my story while you read the book.

Unfortunately, due to nature of paper, this isn't possible with the print edition. So, sprinkled throughout the book are URL's to watch the video that coincides with the chapter.

I hope you'll take advantage of these videos. They will not only provide you with further information on how to not suck, but also a window into my life and story.

I look forward to seeing you on the inside.

Ben

INTRODUCTION

Guys, we suck at relationships.

I understand this is a huge assumption. But make no mistake – we struggle to have healthy and vibrant relationships in our lives. How do I know? When was the last time you felt the joy and comfort of a strong community of friends? Are you avoiding someone at work because of a past conflict? Within the last year, have you felt lonely at any point? How is your dating life?

Our culture has taught us that the best way to get ahead is to use and consume people. And we've fallen straight into that trap. It's doing whatever it takes to make our way up the corporate ladder. It's pursuing romantic relationships with the sole purpose of getting the girl into bed. We use others to get what we want, wreaking havoc on their lives without even realizing it. This is the picture of us. People slide in and out of our lives and verify our struggle with relationships.

But our culture isn't entirely to blame. Many of our behaviors are caused by wounds that destroy our relationships. Our wounds eat us from the inside out, causing us to become men none of us ever dreamed of being. What goes on inside of us changes the way our worlds are being shaped. Our inability to harbor and foster healthy relationships runs deep, stunting our growth and hindering our causes, careers, livelihoods and legacies. Because we suck at relationships, we are unable to make a dent in this world like we want to.

The biggest dent you can make in this world, the greatest legacy you can leave on earth, is not found in one single possession or profit gained over years. It's found in people. Never once has an obituary mentioned the possessions a person has collected. They only talk about the people they knew and loved. Your legacy on this earth will always come down to relationships and the people you invest in.

That is what this book is about. This book will help you gain the confidence you need to build stronger relationships so you can truly thrive. It will give you the tools you need to make the dent in this world you've been looking to make. This book will provide the steps, tools and action plans that will make you the hero in your dating life, your friendships, your workspace and your career.

It's time to heal. It's time for us to get better at relationships. It's time for us to take the journey to get the life and legacy we want. It's time for us to stop sucking at relationships. It's time for the world to get the generation of young men it deserves.

I would love to tell you this is going to be easy. I would love to say that it's going to be comfortable. But it's not. My goal, in fact, is to make you feel a little uncomfortable.

In the pages that follow, be prepared to be challenged. You will read things you don't want to read. I'm not going to pull any punches: I want you to get up and move from your current life position and do something about your relationships.

> **Your legacy on this earth will always come down to relationships and the people you invest in.**

Relationships aren't soft like a pillow. They are hard and tricky to step into. For too long, we haven't been willing to become uncomfortable. But when you decide to make this investment in yourself and your relationships, it will change everything. My hope is that as you make this investment, you will be made into a new man. I know – that's a bold statement. But I believe in the power of relationships and what they can do in your life.

So, it's time to get started. Let's get to work.

TO HEAR MORE ABOUT BEN'S STORY HEAD OVER TO: BENWEAVER.ORG/RELATIONSHIPBONUS

YOUR LEGACY ON THIS EARTH WILL ALWAYS COME DOWN TO RELATIONSHIPS.

CHAPTER 1

1
BEGIN LIVING AS IF RELATIONSHIPS ARE EVERYTHING

The road to better relationships is paved through value

I haven't always been the guy calling out men on their relationship issues. My journey began just like yours – with humble beginnings. I have sat where you sit. Broken, frustrated and clueless, I bulldozed over people like it was going out of style. I soon hated the person I had become.

My journey toward healthier relationships began with coming to terms with the people in my past and present. I had to stop buying the cultural lie, treating people as something to be conquered or consumed. I had to come to terms with the fact that people are … well, people. They bear the image of God, they have souls, and they matter. Somewhere along the way, in the midst of my brokenness

and frustration, I had forgotten that. In the end, I concluded people aren't just something in my life.
Instead, people and relationships are *everything*.

It would be nice to get to the practical work right away, wouldn't it? Of course – but what good would it do if your heart and your view of people remained the same? Getting better at relationships begins with your heart. You must change your inner world before you can change your relationships. You must learn to address the pain and hurt that brought you to the place you are now. This will happen over time, through lots of honest conversations with trusted individuals and spiritual disciplines you put into practice every single day. It is a journey worth taking, I promise you.

Understanding relationships as everything is a complete transformation of mind and heart. Do not overlook this. If you skim through this chapter just to get to the practical stuff at the end, you will have missed the whole point. What's waiting for you at the end of this chapter won't work because you haven't done the work here.

People are the greatest investment you can make. It is people who will shape your life. But for you to get what you want (and yes, I will help you with that, too), you must begin believing, living and practicing that relationships are everything. You must value people.

Valuing others isn't easy. Your perception of them must transform for your value of others to grow. You will have to revamp the way you approach others. Your interactions with everyone you encounter will look different. You must set your focus on people.

Where do you begin? With the smallest of conversations. Start by entering those conversations with what you can give rather than what you can take. It's not about offering unsolicited advice – it's about putting the needs and concerns of others before yourself. It's about placing yourself at eye level and considering how you can serve them. It's from those interactions that a foundation for understanding and building healthy relationships come. To live as relationships are everything you must discover the power of giving value in conversation rather than taking it.

I wish someone would have come alongside me years ago and pointed out how I sucked at relationships. While it was never my intent to take from others as I did, it was how I treated people. The largest way in which this played out for me was in how I kept my greatest hurts and struggles from others. I thought if I could keep my weaknesses hidden away then I would be accepted more. Little did I realize in withholding myself I became a taker and consumer of others.

> **To live as relationships are everything you must discover the power of giving value in conversation rather than taking it.**

For me, having a conversation with someone in which I gave more than I took was difficult. All I cared about was getting ahead and conquering the next biggest adventure. My work with others suffered. Resolving conflict became impossible because I didn't know how to share my hurts in fear of appearing weak. I kept people at arm's length. I didn't know how to "do" relationships. It was an awful life I do not want for you.

But over time, something inside me changed. I began to work on my inner world, including the hurts and wounds that kept me from healthy relationships for years. I finally decided to engage in what my heart was screaming. I began by inviting others into my world and let them see what was really going on. All my hurts, struggles and pain out on the table. I learned what it meant to be a giver and follow the trusted advice of friends who had never given up on me.

With the help of others, I pulled myself out of the mess I was in, and my valuation of others changed dramatically. So did my perception of relationships. They were no longer just something – they became everything. I learned the value of others and how important it was to let them into my life.

Putting into practice how I viewed people and relationships made my life better almost overnight. I no longer kept people at a distance. I was more open and honest in conversations. I was intentional in how I carved out time to spend with family and friends. I focused on what I could give in relationships rather than what I could take. I found that when I let them in close to my broken world to find out they, too, faced challenges. It was freeing. I was led to a place of complete humility and increased confidence in my own heart of who God made me to be. I found the way through people – through relationships. But I had to go there. No one could go there for me.

I want to put you on the fast track to accomplish what took me years to figure out. All you must do is grasp this simple idea:

> **RELATIONSHIPS ARE EVERYTHING**

Live by this motto every single day. It will change your world. You will be a different man tomorrow, next week and a year from now. If you're curious to know why relationships are everything, I'll get to that more in chapter three. Keep reading.

START RIGHT NOW:

What do you want this to look like for you? When this is all said and done, what kind of man do you want to be in the end? If you want to remain the same, shutting off people from your life, then stop reading. Go live your life and get the same results you keep getting. You'll end up alone.

But if you want to change – if you want to be a man who values relationships and people in the highest regard, then begin by taking stock of where you're at right now.

At the end of this chapter is a blank page for you to take some notes. Write something down there, in a journal or in a computer document about the relationships in your life and how you want them to look different. I won't look over your shoulder to make sure you are doing the work. You're a big boy. This is on you. If you want to push yourself even further, grab a friend to keep you accountable.

Take stock. Be honest and begin today by valuing people differently than you ever have before.

DO THIS:

1. Take some time to do the exercise mentioned above. Be honest with yourself – where are you at? How do you value others? How can you make your relationships the most important thing in your life?

2. Write down the names of 7-10 people currently in your life and scale how much you value them, with 1 being "I barely value the person or relationship" and 10 being "I focus totally on this person, his/her needs and investing in him/her constantly." Be honest. When you are finished, consider these questions for each person and their rating: Why did you give these people the ratings you did? Do you think they would rate their relationships with you the same way?

3. Choose one person from your list today. Send his/her value through the roof and see what happens.

> **a.** How do you do this? Write a note, send flowers, call – you'll know what to do. You'll know how to bring value to the relationship based on who you choose.

b. Let's just call this out: Yes, I am asking you to do something out of the ordinary and unexpected. Because you currently struggle with relationships, every behavior I ask you to establish moving forward is going to seem weird to others. The weirdness will wear off after a while.

4. Pray. This may sound crazy, but I can tell you that prayer makes a radical difference in my life. Ask God for his help in this process. Ask him to show you people you need to invest in. God is most interested in a relationship with us. This is something he understands and wants us to succeed in. He will guide you.

TO HEAR MORE ABOUT BEN'S STORY HEAD OVER TO: BENWEAVER.ORG/RELATIONSHIPBONUS

BOTTOM LINE:

Begin seeing and valuing people for who they are – image bearers of God with souls who need our care.

NOTES

RELATIONSHIPS AREN'T JUST SOMETHING.

RELATIONSHIPS ARE EVERYTHING.

CHAPTER 2

2
EMBRACE PAIN AS PART OF THE PROCESS

The road to better relationships is paved through pain

You and I understand pain all too well. We experience it every single day, in a variety of ways we often can't explain.

By most standards, pain is something we should absolutely avoid. But there are also times where pain is welcomed. We understand the sacrifice of a little pain for the burn of a good workout and feeling and looking good. We love to grovel in the pain after doing something epic with our friends. We'll even go on for days about the stories behind the scars we carry on our bodies.

But pain, even chased after for pleasure, isn't easy. If we're honest, most of us avoid pain, and what it may represent for our ego, at all costs. Many of us would wait until our arm is falling off before admitting we are in pain. The inner drive for men to be noticed and honored despite almost missing an arm is more appealing than acknowledging the pain that comes along with it.

Let's get real. Losing an arm isn't too common these days. But holding onto our pride for the sake of not appearing to be hurt is.

The manifestation of pain

Pain manifests itself in a wide variety of ways. What comes to mind quickly is physical pain. This is the pain we pay close attention to because it affects how we go about our day.

But physical pain isn't the pain we avoid the most. The pain men avoid most is emotional. It's the pain we feel when people hurt us with their words. We feel it when conflict boils over between us and another person. It's the emptiness we feel from loneliness. Emotional pain is what we feel when we're not in control. It runs straight to the heart and doesn't go away easily. Emotional pain manifests itself in relationships every day, and we avoid it like the plague.

Why we avoid pain

We avoid pain because we're not interested in getting hurt. If we allow ourselves to get hurt, there is potential for all sorts of repercussions – anxiety, fear, depression and even more hurt. When you or I experience emotional pain or hurt, we get this feeling that life just got real. It's not all Skittles and rainbows anymore. We suddenly learn that brokenness is a part of life. Therefore, we avoid emotional pain at all costs. Who would want to endure all I just mentioned?

But here's the interesting thing about pain in relationships. We need it. We not only need it, it is part of the foundation for fostering healthy relationships in our lives. Without pain, we cannot have growing relationships with others. It sounds crazy and backward, but you and I need to begin running toward and embracing potential pain in the relationships we invest in.

This is where it gets difficult. Embracing pain doesn't sound practical. So, what does it look like? It's handling conflict with someone at work when you can easily turn the other way and bury it. It's apologizing to a friend you wounded deeply. It's forgiving a family member who hurt you years ago. It is you embracing pain of all shapes and sizes in hopes of restoring a relationship. Embracing pain is deciding to do something about your emotions and handling them properly rather than writing them off.

> **Without pain, we cannot have growing relationships with others.**

Not all of our relationships produce pain. But more pain lingers in our lives than we care to admit. It's buried deep inside of us, and we need to address it. When we understand the power of embracing pain and absorbing it as it comes along, it will only make our relationships stronger.

We have sucked at relationships for too long partly because we haven't been willing to address and embrace pain in our relationships. To grow the confidence we need to build strong relationships and make a dent in this world, we must embrace pain and potential hurt as a part of the process.

WHAT DOES IT MEAN TO LEAN INTO PAIN?

Understand pain's part in the process.

Knowing pain is part of relationships is half the battle. G.I. Joe would be proud! When you approach others knowing you might experience hurt and pain along the way, it changes everything.

I'm not suggesting you are going to get hurt. What I am telling you is embracing pain is healthy, and you must learn to become vulnerable to it.

Some of my deepest friendships have stemmed from pain – either that I've caused or that the other person has caused. Pain is a part of humanity we must learn to embrace. We will hurt each other. But in our hurt, we can also learn from and grow with each other.

Understand the power of self-sacrifice.

We don't understand or practice sacrifice anymore. What men view as drive or passion others see as self-centeredness, egocentrism or an unwillingness to give to others. We've forgotten what it means to put others first and ourselves further down the line. This must give.

> ### *"So the last will be first and the first will be last." — Jesus*

How are you with that little statement above? Don't get hung up about the implications of who it came from. Focus on the 12 important words making it up. If your tongue isn't stuck in your throat at this very moment, you may want to do a heart check. We don't care to understand or practice statements like these anymore because they don't benefit us.

True relationships – healthy, growing and vibrant relationships – are self-sacrificing. They are self-LESS. Men who practice self-sacrifice put others first and themselves last. For us as young men, there is no greater way we can do this than by serving and sacrificing for our families in our current season of life. While each of our family situations are uniquely different, the ways in which we can serve them are similar. You can get started in this selfless attitude by simply making yourself available.

One of the more selfish things I did as a young single man in my twenties was not being around when others needed me. Do better than me. Make yourself available to those who love and care for you. Availability is the first step towards self-sacrifice.

Men who have learned to practice availability have surrendered themselves to the greater good of the relationship. They have chosen to embrace the pain in the relationship, no matter the cost. And let's be honest – self-sacrifice is painful. It isn't easy, but it's necessary to get the life you want.

Understand that true adventure is found in pain.

If you were to share with me one of the greatest adventures of your life, I'd be willing to bet it involved pain along the way.

Your thoughts, memories and even pain last longer than feelings of joy and delight. They leave scars. But scars have purpose. They remind us that despite all we went through, it was worth it. The adventure you experienced made the pain more worth it. As men, we take ourselves through the grueling process of pain in everything – work, sports, you name it. All in the hopes of finding ourselves better on the other side.

The same is true in relationships. When you endure and embrace pain, you become a better man for it.

We avoid pain partly because we believe we are the only

men who will ever experience it. This is simply not true. If you begin paying attention to relationships in your life, you will find a world of pain that others are experiencing. But you've got to go there to experience it.

Do not forget this ever-important truth: You are not alone. Other men are taking this journey with you. The enemy will try to convince you that you are the only one experiencing it. He's lying to you. We're in this together, and that will never change.

> **Through pain we experiece others in ways we could not have otherwise. Through pain we become the men we are supposed to be. Through pain we become the men others long for us to be.**

TO HEAR MORE ABOUT BEN'S STORY HEAD OVER TO: BENWEAVER.ORG/RELATIONSHIPBONUS

DO THIS:

1. Take a moment and write down three relationships you currently have or want to have, and give one specific reason why it might be painful to step further into these relationships. Maybe there is a conflict or potential for rejection. Your reasoning could be as simple as, "I don't want to make the investment. It's too uncomfortable." It's cool. I won't throw you over the edge just yet. We'll get there, though.

2. Pick one relationship that may involve pain and take one step toward embracing it. Pick up the phone and make a call. Have a sit-down. Do what you need to do on your end to show humility and make it right. Often pain will soften when we humble ourselves.

3. Consider praying about your pain. Some of us have deep-rooted pain we are unsure how to handle. Take it before God and ask him how you can learn from the pain.

BOTTOM LINE:

Pain is real. For you to experience relationships the way you want, you will have to embrace pain.

NOTES

PAIN IS A PART OF THE PROCESS.

HALF TIME

HALF TIME

Congratulations. You've made it halfway. You need to know how significant this is. You are now more likely to finish. It's true. Most people, when they know they've gone halfway, won't turn around and go back. They will finish. That is exactly what you are going to do. You're going to finish.

Let's do a quick recap before we move on. So far you should have gained an entirely new perspective on relationships.

Don't forget: Relationships aren't just something. Relationships are everything.

You've also picked up on the idea that entering into relationships as God designed them is going to cause pain.

Don't forget: You are not alone in the pain. Lean into it. Everyone else experiences it, too.

It's time to join the rest of the world and experience what real relationships look like. It's now time to keep moving forward. It's time to change the way you live and breathe in your relationships. This is the everyday, grind-it-out kind of stuff. Everything you read before was internal processing. We needed to address the heart. What you read moving forward will help you flesh all of this out in your relationships.

How will you begin treating your family?
Your girlfriend?
Your friends?
Your co-workers?
What will your relationship with God look like?

You will have these questions answered when you're done. No, I'm not going to give you all the answers, so there's no need to skip ahead. You'll have to find those on your own. The chapters following will require some hard work. But you're good for it.

Did I not say that before? My bad. Relationships are work. This is just how it goes. Relationships are work because people are work. People (yes – you, too) are work because they are complicated. There is no way around it.

Halftime is over. Keep pressing in. Don't stop at any cost. This isn't easy, but it's worth every moment. Let's keep moving.

CHAPTER 3

3

STOP CONSUMING PEOPLE START INVESTING IN THEM

The road to better relationships is paved through investing

Within the last 70 years, America's economy has boomed with consumerism. Now in the 21st century, we have formed a full-on consumer culture. Products such as water are packaged, marketed and sold to people who are interested in drinking from the mountains of factories in which we create a better version of H2O.

Getting anything you want for the price you want builds the consumer mindset we all think is easy to shake. But we can't. When we are told we can have more, we instantly want more. If we can get what we want faster, we'll take it. If we can become the success we've all dreamed of overnight, we'll go to any cost to achieve it. Bigger. Faster. Stronger.

We have created a recipe for disaster. Men are the guiltiest of these desires. While there is nothing wrong with consuming, the story shifts when our stuff begins to own us. As a result, we have become enslaved to the culture we have created. We are no longer free to be the men we want to be or are supposed to be. We suffer because of our enslavement, and others around us suffer, too.

Take a moment and feel the weight of this. You and I cannot be the men we want or need to be because we have bought into – and become enslaved to – a culture telling us we can get whatever we want, when we want.

Here is why this is a problem: We have turned people into a consumable.

Do not skip over this. Think about how this is happening in your life. You and I treat people as if they are something to be consumed.

"What can I get from you?"

We may never utter those words, but our hands and hearts practice them every single day in our interactions with the people we work with, hang out and spend time with. After we get what we want we dispose of the rest.

- Money
- Possessions
- Achievements
- Promotions
- Sex

We consume each of these in our own selfish ways and move on. You can add "people" to the list, too.

This should make us sick.

This old breed of selfishness found its way into our new world when we began to treat relationships as products, rather than people who are to be invested in. Relationships became more about what we can take rather than what we can give.

Do not forget what you've learned thus far: The dent you leave in this world begins and ends with people. Stuff is stuff, and money is all right, but they are never more important than people.

As we push forward, hang on to this truth:

NO ONE wants or deserves to be treated like stuff to be consumed.

I hope you're listening. And I hope you're dialed in at this point, because you should be. Let's talk about how to fix this problem.

HOW TO MAKE THE TURN FROM CONSUMING OTHERS TO INVESTING IN THEM.

Re-establish the value and importance of people.

At the beginning of this book, I shared about the value of others and how important this idea is in fostering healthy relationships. It's key for you to understand why this is so important.

People bear the image of God. In all shapes, sizes, colors and races, every person who has ever walked the face of this earth has been designed and created in the image of God. This idea is crucial in helping you build healthy relationships with others. If you can gain a new perspective and respect others for who they are and how God made them, it will change everything.

Being created in the image of God is an idea that makes our heads hurt. We can't fully wrap our brains around it. But this doesn't change the validity of the idea. God's plan in Genesis 1 of the Bible is to create. He makes everything out of nothing. He speaks, and what you and I see in our world comes into existence. It's mind blowing.

Out of everything God creates, there is only one creation he makes in his image: humans. You and me. Your neighbor. Your loved ones, friends and co-workers. Because of God's design, each of us carries the image and fingerprint of God in a unique way. Nothing else bears his image.

This should radically change the way we view others. The reason we treat others as image bearers of God is the same reason you and I want to be treated this way – we are image bearers, too.

But here is the most interesting part about this idea: I can't change how you view others. I wish I could, but I can't. See, there is no statement of words I can put together to implant this idea in your heart and help you live it out every day. The only step I will challenge you to take in this moment is to allow God in and let him transform you. This is the only way your perspective and value of others will change.

But don't wait on God. Yes, he will be quick, but if you want to believe this, then DO it. This is how you are changed. You begin putting it into practice NOW. If you want to value people for who God made them to be, don't wait for a warm and fuzzy feeling in your heart. Live out and practice the idea that people are created in God's image, unique and worthy of honor and respect.

Switch your mindset from taking to giving.

The best way to live out this practice is this principle: You must give more than you take. We have become such amazing takers. We bully, push, shove and lord it over people to get what we want. Taking has become easy. We love it because we're good at it. Giving, on the other hand, is much more difficult. In fact, it is one of the most difficult practices to do here on this earth. But here is what is interesting about giving. Giving is a part of the new economy to get ahead.

Now, giving doesn't come easily and without sacrifice, but the science is there. The more you give, the more you will get in return. Apply this to the relationships you need to begin valuing and investing in. It's a complete change of mindset, but one worth exploring. If you want to become successful on any scale in life, you must become a giver –

and giving to others by serving them is the best way to get there. But you'll have to get your hands dirty.

> **"The more I help you, the more successful I become. But I measure success in what it has done for the people around me. That is the real accolade."**
> **—Adam Grant, Give & Take:**
> **A Revolutionary Approach to Success**

Guys, forget what culture is shouting at you. It will continue to tell you that to get in life you must TAKE. Taking will only lead to a path of destruction and loneliness. I've been there. It's ugly.

Get the best life for yourself by giving. Get there by serving others and giving them your best. In a world calling for leaders, serve first. In a world telling you to fight for the front seat, take the back. In a world offering you the best of the best, be OK with just taking second. Be OK with just serving.

Yes, I get how backward this sounds. People may even call you a laughingstock. But the same people laughing are the same investing in stocks that will only offer loneliness for returns.

You've got your chance right now to be a better guy. There's a better way, so take it. Do not pursue gain in this life at the expense of others. Regain a new value of people. Become a giver. Serve the world with your best. When you learn these simple practices, your investment in others will skyrocket.

TO HEAR MORE ABOUT BEN'S STORY HEAD OVER TO: BENWEAVER.ORG/RELATIONSHIPBONUS

DO THIS:

1. Your heart needs a change. It's time to take a different direction. Ask God to completely redirect and change your heart. This is where your true healing begins. It's bold, but it's life changing.

2. Choose one person from the lists you have created and find a way to invest in that person today or tomorrow. What can you give that will solve a problem for that person? How can you serve in such a way that changes your view of the person? How can you put this person before yourself? Next week, put one or two hours on your calendar to give your time toward a person in some uncanny way. Make sure to make this project about people. Maybe you serve at a food bank or shelter. Maybe you mow your neighbor's lawn. Be creative. Do it and expect nothing in return.

3. There is another great opportunity for prayer here. Ask God to step into your relationships and have you see them the way he does – with their value, gifts, hurts and insecurities all right in front of you.

BOTTOM LINE:

The more you invest in others, the more you will thrive in life, and the bigger your dent will be.

NOTES

STOP CONSUMING PEOPLE. START INVESTING IN THEM.

CHAPTER 4

4

VULNERABILITY IS YOUR MOJO

The road to better relationships is paved through vulnerability

Have you ever had a first date that changed your life? I have. In fact, it is one of the reasons you are reading this today. This date happened over a hot cup of tea (don't judge) spread over a couple of hours of decent conversation before we both went our separate ways, never to see each other again.

My single life has been full of these encounters. So, what made this one life changing? That one conversation sparked a problem in my heart I had to deal with right away. It was causing me to suck at relationships. Something had to give.

A mutual friend set us up. After our date, each of us spoke to him on separate occasions to share the full details of how it all went down. Each of us was curious about the other's thoughts. I am not sure I could have been any more surprised by what my friend shared with me. It came from way out of left field:

She said I lacked vulnerability.

I know what you're thinking: I should have been upset at the observation she made. But I wasn't. In fact, I was relieved when I heard my friend say it.

Up to that point in my life, I couldn't nail down what was wrong with my relationships. I kept thinking other people or circumstances were the problems. But this wasn't true. I was the one to blame.

In two hours over a cup of tea, this young woman put to words something my heart had been screaming for a long time. I was lonely and strung out on blaming others for why I had become the person I was. I was the one with the problem. I kept others at arm's length, unwilling to open myself to others and experience real life.

My story is yours

Chances are, if you are reading this you can relate to what you just read. Like me, you may not have been able to put your finger on why exactly you suck at relationships.

It's vulnerability. Guys, I promise you. It's this. We suck at being vulnerable with people. To step into a thriving life of healthy relationships and make a dent in this world, you must become vulnerable. One of the greatest investments you can make in your own life, beginning today, is to come to a place where vulnerability is championed and welcomed.

If you want a better life for yourself, champion vulnerability. If you want a better life for others, champion vulnerability.

So, what exactly is vulnerability?

Simply defined, vulnerability is this: the quality or state of being exposed to the possibility of being attacked or harmed, either physically or emotionally.

> **"Vulnerability sounds like truth and feels like courage."**
> **— Brené Brown, *Daring Greatly***

We don't have to venture far into that definition before we feel the need to stay away. We don't enjoy words such as "exposed," "attacked" or "harmed." Even words tied to emotion don't get us all too excited. Vulnerability requires the opportunity to be exposed to hurt. We don't want to be hurt.

We've done this to ourselves. We have bought into a culture where image and appearances are king and vulnerability makes us appear weak. To even appear weak makes men of all shapes and sizes feel inadequate. Our love for how we look and feel on the outside dictates who we are becoming in our hearts – cold, shut off and broken men. It has affected the deepest places of our hearts and has now made its way into the lives we claim to love and care for.

What we have been believing and practicing out of fear of weakness or hurt is backward. The weakness now evident in our relationships has exposed us for who we have become – weak men in a society in desperate need of men who step into fear, not away from it.

We have become men who don't take risks in life because we are afraid of failing or appearing inadequate. Something must change if we are going to step into life every day becoming the men we want to be.

The life we need to pursue

We were designed to live full lives. For us, this begins with understanding and practicing vulnerability. It is our greatest strength in moving forward in any relationship.

Stepping into a relationship with the potential of harm and appearing weak takes guts. It takes strength. It isn't cowardly. Stepping into weakness, fear and harm fulfills the desire of every man to achieve something great. It is daring greatly in the arena of life. It's leaving everything out on the arena floor, knowing you gave it all.

"It is not the critic who counts; not the man who points out how the strong man stumbles, or where the doer of deeds could have done them better. The credit belongs to the man who is actually in the arena, whose face is marred by dust and sweat and blood; who strives valiantly; who errs, who comes short again and again, because there is no effort without error and shortcoming; but who does actually strive to do the deeds; who knows great enthusiasms, the great devotions; who spends himself in a worthy cause; who at the best knows in the end the triumph of high achievement, and who at the worst, if he fails, at least fails while daring greatly, so that his place shall never be with those cold and timid souls who neither know victory nor defeat."

— Theodore Roosevelt, *Citizens in a Republic*

Be the man who gets into the arena and gives his all in everything in life, not just in his career, work or life's pursuits. Give your all to the people who will help you make a dent in this world. Do this by becoming vulnerable. Dust, sweat, blood and all. For you to thrive and have healthy relationships, vulnerability will need to be your mojo. You will have to step into fear and harm, not away from it.

A life lacking vulnerability isn't open. It isn't honest, receptive or caring. It isn't worthy of the heart of another. It is a lonely life. But a life drenched in vulnerability is a heart wide open. It is ready to receive at the risk of being harmed. This is a life to be cherished. Guys, this is the heart you want.

HOW DO WE BECOME MORE VULNERABLE AND SPARK CHANGE?

Be more courageous toward others.

This is more than just standing up for yourself. Step out in courage in the relationships you want to pursue. Fight for relationships you long to have. Refuse to give in. Do this with a gentle heart and you will get further, faster with others. But you have to step out.

Show gratitude.

Learn to become a grateful person, and you will become a more open, honest and real person, too.

Something about remembering who and what we have brings life back into perspective and gives us what we need – joy. Learn to embrace the joy of what you have and what is now.

Stop chasing the perfectionist shiny ball.

Sure, it's fun to chase after the "more fun" and "better" you. But you'll get tired fast. The more quickly you stop chasing perfection, the shorter road you'll have to becoming a more vulnerable and wholehearted individual. Just be yourself.

Seek to belong, not just to connect.

It's natural and easy to be connected in this world. There isn't anything wrong with it. But sometimes we settle for connection when we are truly seeking to belong. When we seek to belong rather than just connect, we seek to be a part of something in which we can be ourselves, not someone else.

This is what you are looking for in life. Connections are a dime a dozen. Belonging comes along in rare form and is what makes us the people we want to become. Belonging is where vulnerability thrives.

TO HEAR MORE ABOUT BEN'S STORY HEAD OVER BENWEAVER.ORG/RELATIONSHIPBONUS

DO THIS:

1. Find someone this week you are close with and have a conversation about vulnerability. Have no other agenda but that. Ask where this person thinks you are at – and ask this person to be deathly honest. If you are having a hard time finding someone to talk to, there's a good chance you need some work on this one.

2. Find a way this week to show an immense amount of gratitude toward someone. It may be someone you have wanted to thank for a while. Wait no longer. Do it now.

3. Find a way to make your cracks show in a funny way. It is never easy to be self-effacing in public. Do something this week to show others who you are – and be funny about it. Don't be stupid or illegal, but make it memorable to those you love. You must learn to laugh at yourself.

4. A prayer of vulnerability or courage is not one to be taken lightly. Ask God to give you the courage you need this week to step into healthy but often hard conversations and relationships.

BOTTOM LINE:

Healthy relationships come at the cost of being vulnerable, but it will always be a cost worth bearing.

NOTES

VULNERABILITY IS YOUR MOJO.

CONCLUSION

Your journey has just begun. Mine is continuing. I'm still learning what it means to live in, foster and build healthy relationships in my life. But I can tell you one thing for sure as you come to the close of this book: This is the life you want.

Don't get cocky yet. The finish line of this guide on relationships isn't the end of your journey of not sucking at them. It's just the beginning. But here is what is great about finishing this book. You will have a blueprint to move forward. I will even go as far as to say you will be well on your way toward the remodel of your life. You can come back to these plans time and time again when you need to make some adjustments. Come back anytime. The tools and practices are here.

Speaking of practice ... if you practice this entire book, you will become a new man. The world won't even see you coming. I know because it happened to me. I am Exhibit A. Learn from my mistakes. Put in the hard work and don't take shortcuts.

I promise – all of what you just read is foundational in understanding the power of relationships in your life. It is the beginning of you making a dent in this world. This is how you get the legacy you want. Let me offer you one last piece of advice:

START NOW

This cannot be overstated. We have become who we are because we put things off. Don't do it tomorrow. You haven't been given tomorrow. You have been given today. Tomorrow is full of bad habits, behaviors and practices because you didn't start today. Tomorrow is where you still suck at relationships. Today you can start not to.

We must do better. Your call to action moving forward is to put into practice all you have read. Don't let it overwhelm you, but do begin somewhere. Starting today means by the time this day is over you will be on your way to becoming a better man.

To keep yourself accountable, invite others into the process. Talk to your friends, your girlfriend, your family. Share this book with them. Put them on notice – not only do you want to be better at relationships, but you are going to do whatever it takes to get there.

You are on your way.

Thanks for reading. Thanks for digging in. Thanks for believing in yourself and realizing that you no longer have to suck at relationships. There's a better life waiting, and you are on your way toward it.

Stay engaged in this community. If there is anything you need, reach out. It's why I'm here.

ABOUT THE AUTHOR

Ben earned his master's degree in Christian Education/Theology from Dallas Theological Seminary. He is a native of St. Louis, where he has served as a Youth Pastor since 2011 and currently lives with his golden retriever, Gracie. He loves adventure, good music, long bike rides, snowboarding trips with the guys, tacos with his incredible girlfriend, and donuts.

Ben believes the world deserves a better generation of men, and he wants to help give it to them. His mission is simple -- to help guys reclaim the confidence they need to build strong relationships and make their dent in this world.

He muses about all of this over here...

http://www.facebook.com/bweave
http://www.twitter.com/b_weave
http://www.instagram.com/b_weave
http://benweaver.org

NOTES

NOTES

NOTES

NOTES

RELATIONSHIPS ARE EVERYTHING 14-DAY ACTION PLAN

INTRO: **Getting Practical**

After I finished Relationships Are Everything, there was a question others who had read the first edition kept asking me - "How can you make this more practical?" Of course, there is the action steps at the end of each chapter which are equally crucial to the book, but could there be more? Is there an opportunity to not just create something applicable but to create habits in each of our lives that will help us form stronger relationships every single day?

After more dreaming and collaborating, I came up with what you see the next several pages. A complete, 14-day action plan that will get you started on your journey to make sure relationships aren't just something, but everything in your pursuit of this life you want, knowing that it will be your relationships which get you there.

The pages that follow is a more extensive look at how far you can get down the road with relationships when you are highly focused and intentional about them. In turn, when you can focus on your relationships, your life, as a whole, will look better. It just will. If you take this seriously, the outcome will change everything.

My hope for you is as you look through the lens of people and relationships it will help you to plan your life, career, and legacy. It will spark a change in your life not many people will experience. You can count on that.

Now, how do I know that? Relationships are hard work. We've already discussed this. And people aren't always willing to do the hard work it takes to get their relationships in order.

I want to help you succeed, so there is one more step you can take to help you obtain the healthy relationships you need.

At the bottom of this page, there is a website you can visit to subscribe to a weekly e-mail that I will drop directly into your inbox that will provide fresh tips, action steps and accountability in helping you to become better at relationships.

To subscribe, simply head here:

www.benweaver.org/relationships

Let's get started. Each day has a small challenge of its own, and I don't want to waste any time in getting you there. The life you want is waiting for you on the other side.

DAY ONE:

WHAT KIND OF LIFE DO YOU WANT?

What kind of life do you want? I know - it's a pretty loaded question, isn't it? Loaded, but powerful. A while back I was sitting across from a 19-year-old young man who couldn't answer the question. Up to that point in his life, all he had ever known was heartache, trauma, and brokenness. He believed the rest of his life was going to be the same. "Life? What life?", was his response to me. For him, all he believed that followed was more hell.

Maybe you're him. I hope that isn't the case. Either way, I offer you the same question I proposed to him - what kind of life do you want? I didn't let him off the hook, and I'm not going to let you off either. So, here's what I want you to do with space below. I want you to write a few sentences (or more, there are note pages all over this book) of the kind of life you want. Here's the trick to this exercise, though. I want you to write the first thing that comes to your mind. You likely already have thoughts. Write them down before you lose them.

As you write, be sure to include at least five elements of the life you want. Write about the career you want, family, things you would like to achieve and focuses you want your life to have. Think along those lines but know there are no limits here. No one is going to glance at your sheet or ever see it and laugh at you. Dream big. Dream very, very big.

(Estimated time, 10-15 minutes)

THE LIFE I WANT:

_____

_____

_____

_____

_____

_____

_____

_____

_____

_____

_____

DAY TWO:

YOU'LL NEED PEOPLE TO GET YOU THERE

If there is anything I want you to take out of this book and action plan and learn from me, it is this: relationships are the most powerful and needed commodity on the planet. They are. If you want to get anything out of this life, then you better think about the relationships you want.

Here is your task, today. Write down the relationships you want in this life. Be very specific here. Name names if you can. Now, if you are single and want to be married, "A Wife" will suffice. If you happen to know the name of the woman you plan on marrying but haven't met her yet, please tell us single guys where you found that superpower.

These could be many relationships - a mentor, friend, or a particular family member. Name the people you want in your life. If you are running up against a wall thinking of people, that's ok. Your goal here is to be as specific as possible. I want you to visualize your life as you are walking through this. (Estimated Time, 10 minutes)

RELATIONSHIPS I WANT:

DAY THREE:

WRITE THE SECOND DRAFT

Our first words are never our best. When we begin writing down what we want, it's good to give it a couple of days to cook inside of us. We need to process it. This processing is especially accurate if you haven't done this before.

I hope by now you have not just written your first draft, but have taken a look at it at least one more time after finishing it. If you haven't, go ahead and do that now.

I now want you to write a second draft, re-framing the 5 (or more) elements of your life that you want. But here is the kicker. I want you to now use people as the basis for the vision you are writing. Think about those relationships that you wrote about yesterday. Consider them as you put words down on this paper and place them at the center of what you are writing.

Why is this important? Because when I asked you what kind of life you wanted, more than likely you chose to write down ideas that are very centered on you. It's ok. Everyone does it. I did it. There isn't anything wrong with it. That first draft is always important. You needed to see an unedited version of the life you want.

Now, I want you to take a look at your life from a broader perspective that is your own. You need to see your life with others included. Without others, your life won't happen the way you planned it.

Don't worry about fitting every relationship into your life plan. I want you to be more mindful than anything that the life you want - the life you need - is at the dead center of relationships (Estimated time: 20-30 min.)

_____

_____

_____

_____

_____

_____

_____

_____

_____

_____

_____

DAY FOUR:

WHO GETS YOUR ATTENTION?

Who are the people in your life that get your attention? Who are the influencers, athletes, celebrities, etc. that dominate your social media feeds? Who are the people that when you look at their life, you say to yourself, under your breath or in your mind "I want a life like that."?

Relationships which go both ways are necessary. They are vital to our life taking off. But sometimes it's people we only watch from a distance that makes the most significant impact on us. These are the blogs you read, podcasts you listen to, videos you watch or people you follow on social media you may never meet. We can call them distant mentors.

Who are those people and why do you want to have a life like theirs? Take a moment and record some of those names below. If you don't have anyone you are paying attention to your next step is to go out on that search and find out who those people are. You are paying attention to more people than you think.

Use the space below to write names and make observations.

(Estimated Time: 10 minutes)

WHO GETS MY ATTENTION?

DAY FIVE:

REVIEW YOUR WORK

It's time for a review of all the work you have done so far. Way to go in making this far. It's not by accident, but with great purpose, you are here. Everything you have done and are about to do with these days will also be with intent, so get ready.

Before we press on, I want you to take a look at where you are at in this process. Take a look at all of the relationships you have written down - those close to you and those far away. How many do you have? If you have more than 15, I want you to cut a few out. Do you have five or less? Dig deep and brainstorm more relationships you want to have in your life.

Let me make a quick caveat before I give you your steps for today. If you are having trouble identifying relationships you want to invest in, I want you to remember two things: 1. You are not alone. This problem is not uncommon with people who have sucked at relationships. I could have quickly raised my hand to this years ago if asked the same question. Don't fret. You've got this. 2. Take notice of how you feel and decide you are going to fix it moving forward.

One of the reasons I would have raised my hand to not having relationships is because I was very self-centered and selfish at specific points in my life. I couldn't identify relationships because I was so focused on me. Maybe that is where you are. Either way, before moving forward do the hard work of finding people who you want to invest energy.

Back to the exercise. For the scope of this review and experiment I want you to get yourself down to 10-15 relationships that you can pour some intentional investment.

Your task is simple - review your relationships, add or take away and adjust your list appropriately.

_____

_____

_____

_____

_____

_____

_____

_____

_____

DAY SIX:

GETTING SMALL & PRACTICAL, ONE RELATIONSHIP AT A TIME.

Building healthy and authentic relationships with those around us doesn't happen overnight. It doesn't even happen over the course of weeks or months. Relationships need time to cook. It's important you start with a small investment that if you keep contributing to will grow over time and you won't get burned out in the process.

Our tendency when we begin pursuing something we are excited or passionate about is to go big. My challenge to you is that for this relationship wisdom to take root and work for the rest of your life, you will need to start in small doses.

Here is your next task. For the next several days (& pages) you are going to focus on one relationship that is on your list from day 3. With every new day brings a new person to invest. Your task is simple. Choose any one from your list and make one investment in them. At least one. Your only guideline is I want you to pick a person from your list that will be able to respond to the investment you made in their life.

Don't over think this. Your investment in this person could be a simple "Thank You" for something they gave or invested in you recently. What is important here is I want you to feel the weight and dialogue of how people affect our drive in life. Others play a crucial role in how we pursue life on our terms, whether we choose to admit it or not. This is what I want you to experience.

As you make your investment, be sure to make it specific to that person and then write your action of what you did in the pages that follow. After recording what you did, write down how you felt when you did it. This step is crucial. Don't skip this step. You'll need your observations later.

Not every person will make you feel great. They may make you feel bitter, angry, jealous or a wide variety of emotions. What is important here is that you record whatever emotion that is.

You have a week's worth of people and pages here. Take the next seven days, starting today and begin putting this investment piece into play. I'll see you in a week.

If you want or need more accountability, find it right here: ***www.benweaver.org/relationships***

Subscribe and get exclusive access to my tips, advice and accountability you won't find anywhere else.

DAY SIX:

INVESTMENT #1

Name of the person: _____

The investment I made: _____

_____

_____

_____

_____

_____

_____

_____

_____

_____

How did you feel after they responded? Write more than a word or two. Sit and think about it.

Why do you suppose you feel the way you did?

_____

_____

_____

_____

_____

_____

What do you want this relationship to look like moving forward? Be honest.

_____

_____

_____

_____

_____

_____

_____

_____

_____

DAY SEVEN:

INVESTMENT #2

Name of the person: _____

The investment I made: _____

_____

_____

_____

_____

_____

_____

_____

_____

_____

_____

_____

How did you feel after they responded? Write more than a word or two. Sit and think about it.

Why do you suppose you feel the way you did?

_____

_____

_____

_____

_____

What do you want this relationship to look like moving forward? Be honest.

_____

_____

_____

_____

_____

_____

_____

_____

DAY EIGHT:

INVESTMENT #3

Name of the person: _____

The investment I made:_____

_____

_____

_____

_____

_____

_____

_____

_____

_____

How did you feel after they responded? Write more than a word or two. Sit and think about it.

Why do you suppose you feel the way you did?

_____

_____

_____

_____

_____

_____

What do you want this relationship to look like moving forward? Be honest.

_____

_____

_____

_____

_____

_____

_____

_____

_____

DAY NINE:

INVESTMENT #4

Name of the person: _____

The investment I made: _____

_____

_____

_____

_____

_____

_____

_____

_____

_____

How did you feel after they responded? Write more than a word or two. Sit and think about it.

Why do you suppose you feel the way you did?

_____

_____

_____

_____

_____

_____

What do you want this relationship to look like moving forward? Be honest.

_____

_____

_____

_____

_____

_____

_____

_____

_____

DAY TEN:

INVESTMENT #5

Name of the person: _____

The investment I made: _____

_____

_____

_____

_____

_____

_____

_____

_____

_____

How did you feel after they responded? Write more than a word or two. Sit and think about it.

Why do you suppose you feel the way you did?

_____

_____

_____

_____

_____

_____

What do you want this relationship to look like moving forward? Be honest.

_____

_____

_____

_____

_____

_____

_____

_____

_____

DAY ELEVEN

INVESTMENT #6

Name of the person: _____

The investment I made: _____

_____
_____
_____
_____
_____
_____
_____
_____
_____
_____
_____
_____

How did you feel after they responded? Write more than a word or two. Sit and think about it.

Why do you suppose you feel the way you did?

_____

_____

_____

_____

_____

What do you want this relationship to look like moving forward? Be honest.

_____

_____

_____

_____

_____

_____

_____

_____

DAY TWELVE:

INVESTMENT #7

Name of the person: _____

The investment I made:_____

_____

_____

_____

_____

_____

_____

_____

_____

_____

_____

How did you feel after they responded? Write more than a word or two. Sit and think about it.

Why do you suppose you feel the way you did?

_____

_____

_____

_____

_____

What do you want this relationship to look like moving forward? Be honest.

_____

_____

_____

_____

_____

_____

_____

_____

_____

DAY THIRTEEN:

WHAT IS CHANGING?

You've been at this now for seven days. Way to go. Most people aren't disciplined to make this happen, but you are. Don't overlook that as you move through this process. Discipline and intentionality are vital in helping to form healthy relationships.

We're not quite to habit status yet, but I want you to start reflecting on what has come of this little relationship experiment so far. Within the last 13 days, you have looked at your life, declared what you want, made others the focus and have been intentional about investing yourself in those people.

Understand how huge this is. You are breaking the scale of importance. My hope for you is a year from now you will look back on this small little journey and know that these were the days that your relationships and life began to change.

I also hope you are beginning to see the power that relationships and people have over us whether we realize it or not. I want you to see you can harness that power and influence for good and not for selfish, manipulative or evil means. If you can take your ability to connect with others and focus on them rather than yourself, you will, in turn, make your life better. Strong and healthy relationships, when intentionally focused on will help you to become the person you were created to be.

Here is what I want to invite you to do today: Write down what you are feeling and what has changed so far. This step is the reason why I had you record how you felt after each interaction and investment with others. You can now recall that information and come to accurate conclusions about where you are at with your emotions. Use the space below to do so.

_____

_____

_____

_____

_____

_____

_____

_____

_____

_____

DAY FOURTEEN:

WASH.
RINSE.
REPEAT.

It's been two weeks since you started this journey of making your relationships a little better, stronger and healthier. You began on day one by creating the life of your dreams - the life you want. I then had you take an inventory of the relationships you'll need to get you there. From there, you revised the life you wanted and threw in distant relationships and mentors of people you want to model your life after. You then went on a seven-day journey where each day you focused on one relationship and zeroed in on its importance in your life. After completing that task, you did some honest reflecting, and I hope your life looks better now than it did two weeks ago. Here is your final charge on this 14-day journey:

DON'T STOP.

The tendency after we finish something is to celebrate (and you should) and then mark the task completed in our minds and move onto what is next. Please don't do this. For the sake of others, the relationships you have begun to reclaim and most importantly you - don't do this.

Right here, right now, where you are no longer kept accountable or given a task to do is where the rubber meets the road. You've only begun. Relationships take a lot of investments made over time.

Your task moving forward from today is simple:

WASH.
RINSE.
REPEAT.

Take everything you just did in that week-long intensive and do it over and over again. Go back to those same relationships, find some new ones and make investments over and over again.

Do whatever it takes to make this happen. Set a reminder on your phone. Put a sticky note on your computer. Keep this task of investment out in front of you, and you will make lightyear jumps in your relationships.

If you would like one more layer of action and accountability, take it now. Head over to:

www.benweaver.org/relationships

Subscribe and get exclusive weekly access to my tips, advice and accountability you won't find anywhere else and will keep you going strong in the relationship game. I'm here if you need me. Don't hesitate to reach out.

Made in the USA
Columbia, SC
24 March 2018